KINGS AND QUEENS

For Cindy

KINGS AND QUEENS

of England and Britain

Roy Charles

Research

Reeva Charles

Illustrations

Kate Evans

QUALITY POCKET BOOKS

www.qualitypocketbooks.com

QUALITY POCKET BOOKS

www.qualitypocketbooks.com

ISBN 978-1-9998981-3-7

A Quality Pocket Book production for:

White On Black Publishing Ltd 2021
Provident House, Burrell Row
Beckenham, Kent BR3 1AT

First Published in the United Kingdom in 2018

THIRD EDITION

Also by the same author:

British Prime Ministers
From 1721 to Brexit

British Castles and Palaces

British Battles
From 825 to the present

Great British Women

Printed in Wales by
Gomer Press Ltd.
for White On Black Publishing,
Parc Menter Llandysul
Llandysul, Ceredigion
SA44 4JL

Design and artwork by
The Workshop
Prescott Cottage
Old Hill, Longhope
Gloucestershire
GL17 0PF

Kings and Queens

Due to historical calendar changes (e.g. from Julian to Gregorian), a mixture of 'old' and 'new' style dates often appear in historical records and sources. I have aimed to use the 'old' style dates where apparent, to reflect the dates recorded at the time.

HOUSE OF WESSEX

Intermittently from 802 to 1066

Originally the West Saxons, the kingdom was founded about AD 500 in the south-west counties of England. Often battling, firstly the Mercians and then the Danes, the Wessex kings were the first to rule over a unitary kingdom of England due to its agrarian wealth and control of south-east England. Finally defeated in 1066 by William the Conqueror, the House of Wessex gave way to the House of Normandy.

SEVENTEEN ENGLISH KINGS ORIGINATED FROM THE WESSEX ROYAL HOUSE:

802–1013

King Egbert (802–39)

King Æthelwulf (839–58)

King Æthelbald (858–60)

King Æthelbert (860–65)

King Æthelred I (865–71)

King Alfred the Great (871–99)

King Edward the Elder (899–924)

King Æthelstan (924–39)

King Edmund I (939–46)

King Edred (Eadred) (946–55)

King Eadwig (Edwy) (955–59)

King Edgar the Peaceful (959–75)

King Edward the Martyr (975–78)

King Æthelred II the Unready (978–1013)

1014–1016 *(restored first time)*

King Æthelred II the Unready (1014–16)

King Edmund II (Edmund Ironside) (1016)

1042–1066 *(restored second time)*

King Edward the Confessor (1042–66)

King Harold II (1066)

King Egbert

b. circa 769–80, d. 839

Reigned 802–39

EGBERT returned from exile abroad in Charlemagne on the death of King Beorthric of Wessex in 802 and succeeded to the West Saxon throne, becoming King of Wessex. He won a decisive victory in 825 at Ellendune (to the south of Swindon) over the Mercian King Beornwulf and went on to defeat the Northumbrian king at Dore near Sheffield.

He is often hailed as the first monarch of England as by 829 he had united England under one monarch for the first time. However, others say this is misleading because, although he managed to briefly issue coins in Mercia in his name, Mercia revolted in 830 and restored its own naïve prince.

Egbert established his son, Æthelwulf, as a 'sub-king' in the south-east while he personally concentrated on other areas. In 838, Egbert went on to defeat the Vikings and their Cornish allies at Hingston Down in Cornwall.

Egbert died in 839 and was succeeded by Æthelwulf. Egbert was buried at Winchester Cathedral, Hampshire. It is believed that during the English Civil War, Parliamentarian soldiers violated Egbert's grave and smashed the windows of the Cathedral with the bones from the royal grave.

He was given the title of 'Bretwalda', Anglo-Saxon for 'ruler of the British'.

KING ÆTHELWULF

b. 795, d. 13 January 858

REIGNED 839–58

ÆTHELWULF succeeded to the throne in 839 on the death of his father, King Egbert (r. 802–39). He was the first son to succeed his father as West Saxon king since 641. Æthelwulf conducted campaigns against the Vikings in Kent in 851 and against the Welsh of Powys in 853. However Æthelwulf was equally interested in religious matters and was generous to churches, granting royal lands to religious foundations.

In 855 Æthelwulf went on pilgrimage to Rome, leaving his son Æthelbald in charge. Æthelwulf was believed to have been accompanied by his six-year-old youngest son Alfred (later 'Alfred the Great'). Away for a year, Æthelwulf returned with a young teenage bride, Judith, daughter of Charles the Bald, the King of West Francia in what is now France. However, from this time until his death, Æthelwulf's authority was confined to the south-east as his son Æthelbald had taken control of Wessex.

Upon his death in 858, and burial at Steyning in Sussex (later transferred to Winchester Cathedral), Æthelwulf was succeeded by his eldest son Æthelbald. King Æthelwulf holds the distinction of being the father of four future kings, including his youngest son, Alfred the Great.

Under Æthelwulf, Old English for 'Noble Wolf', a uniform type of coinage was achieved for all of southern England (except East Anglia).

King Æthelbald

b. circa 831–34, d. 860

Reigned 858–60

ÆTHELBALD succeeded to the throne in 858 after the death of his father, King Æthelwulf (r. 839–58). However, some regard him to have been a 'joint king' with his father for the prior two years: Æthelbald had confined the authority of King Æthelwulf to one area after his father's return from pilgrimage. It is also believed that Æthelbald was part of a plot to prevent his father's return from Rome.

Despite her being his stepmother, Æthelbald married his father's charismatic young widow to capitalise on her own royal lineage: Judith was the daughter of King Charles the Bald, who was King of West Francia (r. 843–77), King of Italy (r. 875–77) and Holy Roman Emperor. However, the marriage faced strong religious opposition as it was considered incestuous and an annulment is said to have been imposed a year later.

Few other details survive of Æthelbald's reign. However, a ninth-century biographer, the Bishop of Sherborne, described it as 'two and a half lawless years' and Æthelbald as 'iniquitous and grasping'.

Æthelbald died in 860 just over two years after succeeding his father and was buried at Sherborne Abbey in Dorset.

His marriage to his stepmother Judith was condemned as 'against God's prohibition and Christian dignity, and also contrary to the practice of all pagans'.

Bishop of Sherborne

King Æthelbert

b. circa 834–36, d. 865–66

Reigned 860–65/6

ÆTHELBERT (meaning 'Noble Bright' in Old English) became King of Wessex in 860 following the death of his brother Æthelbald. He was crowned in Kingston-upon-Thames, as were his father King Æthelwulf (r. 839–58) and brother King Æthelbald (r. 858–60). Æthelbert had previously, since 858, been King of Kent following his father's death. In 860, the first year of his succession, the Danish army landed and attacked Winchester, but were defeated by the Saxons.

In a novel development, Æthelbert included both West Saxon and Kentish people in a new kind of assembly, rather than appointing another member of the family as under-king.

Æthelbert's reign is described as one of good harmony and peace by the Anglo-Saxon Chronicle. While this was true of internal affairs, external forces posed a constant threat. In 865 the Viking 'Great Heathen Army', commanded by Halfdan and Ivar the Boneless, landed in East Anglia and swept across England. By 866, the Vikings had taken York (or Jorvik) and established a North British Kingdom.

King Æthelbert died in 865 or 866 and was buried at Sherborne Abbey in Dorset beside his brother Aethelbald while the kingship passed to his brother Aethelred.

He governed 'in peace, with the love and respect of his subjects'.

ASSER, BISHOP OF SHERBORNE

King Æthelred I

b. circa 847, d. April 871

Reigned 865/6–71

ÆTHELRED (meaning 'Noble Counsel' in Old English) became king on the death of his brother King Æthelbert (r. 860–65/6) and was the third son of his father, King Æthelwulf (r. 839–58) to be crowned. Æthelred's wife is believed to have been Wulfthryth, the daughter or sister of the Ealdorman Wulfhere of Wiltshire. A contemporary charter refers to Wulfthryth as Æthelred's queen, although it was rare at this time for the king's wife to be given this title.

Æthelred's reign was dominated by constant attack by the Danes, who had occupied York in 866. He was defeated by the Vikings at the Battle of Reading on 4 January 871 but four days later defeated them in a clash at Ashdown with much help from his younger brother Alfred. However, in April 871 Æthelred was fatally wounded during the Battle of Meretun in Hampshire. He died soon after, at Witchampton in Dorset.

He was buried at Wimborne Minster (dedicated to St. Cuthberga) in East Dorset and was succeeded by his younger brother, Alfred the Great. Æthelred was known to have two sons, Æthelhelm and Æthelwold, who were too young to succeed their father. Æthelwold was later to dispute the throne with Edward the Elder after Alfred's death in 899.

St. Ethelred, King of the West Saxons.

INSCRIPTION CUT IN THE 1600S ON A BRASS EFFIGY OF THE KING AT WIMBORNE MINSTER

King Alfred the Great

b. 849, d. 26 October 899

Reigned 871–99

ALFRED (meaning 'Elf Counsel' in Old English) became king on the death of his brother King Æthelred and was the fourth of King Æthelwulf's (r. 839–58) sons to have been crowned. Often claimed to be the first King of England, his popularity endures as a 'Great Briton'.

Upon succession, Alfred proved himself to be a cultivated, strong leader winning five years of uneasy peace, during which time London fell to the Vikings in 872. The Vikings invaded Wessex in 878 forcing Alfred to take refuge on Athelney, at that time an island in the Somerset marshes. It is here that the famous 'burning of the cakes' (when he allowed some baking food to burn whilst distracted) is said to have taken place.

However, Alfred managed to lead a defeat of the Vikings at the Battle of Ethandune (Edington) in Wiltshire and the 878 Treaty of Wedmore with Viking leader Guthrum saw Guthrum's baptism and his agreement to retreat to East Anglia. In 885 Alfred went on to impose his rule on South Wales and in 886 took back London. When Guthrum died in 890, Alfred established a permanent army and navy.

Alfred died aged about 50 years old (cause unknown) and was originally buried in the Old Minster in Winchester, although his remains were moved and have become lost over time.

'I desired to live worthily as long as I lived, and to leave after my life, to the men who should come after me, the memory of me in good works.'

King Edward the Elder

b. circa 871–74, d. 17 July 924

Reigned 899–924

EDWARD succeeded his father, King Alfred the Great (r. 871–99), after first successfully dealing with a challenge from his cousin Æthelwold. Soon after, he won a decisive victory against the Danish in East Anglia. In 910 Edward led the defeat of the final Viking army sent to conquer England, winning over their armies at Wessex and Mercia, and recapturing Essex in 913. Edward became ruler of Mercia in 918 when his sister Æthelflaed, the formidable 'Lady of the Mercians', died. Edward continued his father's role in cementing the eminence of Christianity in England.

The Anglo-Saxon Chronicle records that the Scottish King Constantine II submitted to Edward in 923. However, while putting down a Mercian and Welsh revolt in 924, Edward died at Farndon in Cheshire and was buried in the New Minster, Winchester. Edward was believed to have had at least 16 children from three marriages and was succeeded by his eldest son Æthelstan.

Although less information survives about Edward than about his popular father, his legacy is said to be greater than often acknowledged. His ultimate achievement was English unity south of the Humber based on military and institutional success.

He was 'much inferior to his father in the cultivation of letters' but 'incomparably more glorious in the power of his rule'.

WILLIAM OF MALMESBURY

King Æthelstan

b. circa 893–95, d. 27 October 939

Reigned 924–39

ÆTHELSTAN, the son of Edward the Elder (r. 899–924) and his first wife, is believed to have been the first to unite the whole of England under his rule: in 927 he finally conquered York, the last territory remaining under Viking rule.

In 934 Æthelstan invaded Scotland, forcing their king to submit. However, due to resentment by the Scots, in 937 he, together with his half-brother and successor Edmund, led the Battle of Brunanburh which brought them a prestigious victory against a joint force of Scots, Irish and Scandinavians.

Æthelstan is credited with establishing a centralised government and important codes of law, building on the legal reforms of his grandfather, Alfred the Great. He went on to play an important role in European politics, arranging the marriages of several of his sisters with continental royalty.

Æthelstan died in Gloucester and was buried by choice at Malmesbury Abbey, rather than at Winchester with his grandfather, father and brother. It is said this reflected Æthelstan's wish not to honour a city which had opposed his rule and also his devotion to the Abbey.

'Rex Totius Britanniae' – King of all Britain – was minted on his coins.

King Edmund I

b. circa 921–22, d. 26 May 946

Reigned 939–46

EDMUND succeeded his half-brother King Æthelstan (r. 924–39) possibly aged around 17 or 18. He was the son of Edward the Elder (r. 899–924) and his third wife, and also a grandson of Alfred the Great (r. 871–99).

Despite his tender age, he had earned a reputation as a young warrior-prince while fighting fiercely alongside King Æthelstan at the Battle of Brunanburh in 937. Edmund's reign was dominated by conquering and reconquering territories in the north and the Midlands. King Olaf III Guthfrithson had conquered Northumbria and invaded the Midlands. However, the thriving Anglo-Danish communities there reportedly preferred the Christian West Saxon king to the rule of the Scandinavians. Significantly Edmund re-established control over northern England, parts of which had fallen back to the Scandinavians after Æthelstan's death, and reunited England once again.

It is said he had the potential of a great ruler: in addition to his military prowess, he had been involved with King Æthelstan in the establishment of law codes. However, while only in his mid-twenties, it is widely accepted that he was murdered while attending mass in Pucklechurch, Gloucestershire, either by a robber or personal enemy, though some of the details may have been embellished over time.

Edmund's brilliant success won him the name of the 'deed-doer', or to use the modern form of the word – the 'magnificent'.

King Edred (or Eadred)

b. circa 923–24, d. 23 November 955

Reigned 946–55

EDRED, the third son of Edward the Elder to become a West Saxon king, succeeded his murdered brother King Edmund (r. 939–46). As with many of his predecessors, he was faced with battling the Scandinavians. It was not until 954, a year before his death, that Edred defeated and drove out Erik Bloodaxe (King of Norway) who was to be the last ever Danish King of York.

Edred was a devout Christian, leaving large sums of money to relieve poverty and suffering. Unusually his will survives and is held in the British Library.

Edred suffered from ill health due to a stomach ailment; a biographer of the time described how Edred used to suck out the juices of his food. He is believed to have died from this sickness, aged 32, at Frome in Somerset and was buried in the Old Minster at Winchester.

Edred had remained unmarried and brought up his two young nephews as his heirs: Eadwig and Edgar, the sons of King Edmund I. Eadwig succeeded Edred and Edgar later also went on to become King of England.

Edred 'reduced all the land of Northumbria to his control; and the Scots granted him oaths that they would do all that he wanted'.

ANGLO-SAXON CHRONICLE

King Eadwig (or Edwy)

b. circa 940–42, d. 1 October 959

Reigned 955–59

EADWIG, the eldest son of King Edmund (r. 939–46), succeeded to the throne at a young age on the death of his unmarried uncle, King Edred (r. 946–55).

His short rule was dominated by disputes with noblemen and the court clergy. Eadwig's wish to move away from those who had influenced his father and uncle may have been responsible for his exiling of Abbot Dunstan (to whom his uncle was very close). However, another version of events holds that during Eadwig's coronation events, Dunstan had to drag the young king away from 'cavorting' with a woman named Æthelgifu and her daughter. In revenge Dunstan was apparently forced to give up his abbacy of Glastonbury and be exiled.

Aged only 16, Eadwig later married the daughter, Ælfgifu, a third cousin once removed, but the Anglo-Saxon Chronicle reports their forced separation in 958 due to their blood relationship. There is speculation that the annulment was more politically motivated.

Despite the intrigues and brevity of his rule, contemporary sources describe Eadwig as the 'All-Fair' and detail his generosity in giving away land. Eadwig died in Gloucester in 959 (circumstances unknown) and was buried in the New Minster, Winchester.

Known as All-Fair, Edwy 'deserved to be loved'.

His brother-in-law, Æthelweard

KING EDGAR THE PEACEFUL

b. circa 942–44, d. 8 July 975

REIGNED 959–75

EDGAR, the youngest son of King Edmund (r. 939–46), succeeded to the throne on the death of his brother King Eadwig (r. 955–59) after his short rule.

The teenaged Edgar's reign is credited with bringing political stability. Unlike his brother, Edgar surrounded himself with long-serving and trusted advisers including bringing back Dunstan from exile and making him Archbishop of Canterbury. It was Edgar's coronation at Bath in 973 that formed the basis of future coronations.

In a period of lull in Viking activity, Edgar came to be known as 'the Peaceful' for his laws and his recognition of Danish social and legal customs. Edgar worked closely with the Church in a Benedictine reformation which enriched the cultural and educational life of England.

Early in his reign, Edgar was said to have killed a love rival, Earl Æthelwald – an event commemorated by a stone monument, the Dead Man's Plack, erected in 1825 in Longparish, Hampshire.

Edgar died in 975 and was buried at Glastonbury Abbey. In a contested succession, his elder son Edward (possibly illegitimate) was accepted as the next king over Edward's young half-brother Æthelred.

'I will that secular rights stand among the Danes with as good laws as best they may choose. But with the English let that stand which I and my Witan have added.'

King Edward the Martyr

b. circa 962–63, d. 18 March 978

Reigned 975–78

EDWARD was possibly only 12 or 13 when he followed his father to the throne in 975. Edward's succession had been contested by supporters of his legitimate, younger half-brother Æthelred. This led to rival factions emerging within the Church and nobility, almost leading to civil war, and bringing about the later fatal act.

In the third year of his reign, Edward's rule ended abruptly when he was murdered at Corfe Castle in 978 by supporters of his half-brother Æthelred. The cold-blooded stabbing earned him the title of Edward the 'martyr'.

Edward was buried at nearby Wareham without due royal honours, but was later reburied with great ceremony in Shaftesbury Abbey. A cult arose around Edward and he came to be regarded as a saint, with his death date (18 March) set aside as his feast day.

Much later, during Henry VIII's (r. 1509–47) dissolution of the monasteries, Edward's remains were hidden to avoid desecration. Relics recovered in 1931 and then examined in 1970 suggested they may have been Edward's. However, an unresolved dispute about where to relocate them led the relics to be stored for decades in a cutlery box in a bank vault at the Midland Bank in Woking, Surrey.

'No worse deed than this was ever done by the English nation since they first sought the land of Britain. Men murdered him but God magnified him.'

ANGLO-SAXON CHRONICLE

King Æthelred II the Unready

b. circa 966–68, d. 23 April 1016

Reigned 978–1013 (first time)

ÆTHELRED, possibly only aged 10, succeeded to the throne after the murder of his half-brother, King Edward the Martyr (r. 975–78). Following a period of respite from Viking invasion, Danish raids were renewed in the 980s. No military leader, Æthelred was defeated at the Battle of Maldon in 991 and driven to buy off the Danes with immense sums of Danegeld. However, in 1002 Æthelred ordered a massacre of Danish settlers on St. Brice's Day. When King Sweyn Forkbeard of Denmark invaded England in 1013, Æthelred gave up his kingship in favour of Sweyn and at the end of the year fled to Normandy, home of his second wife Emma of Normandy.

Reigned 1014–16 (second time)

King Sweyn's death, just five weeks after he was crowned in December 1013, led to Æthelred being recalled by the English in 1014 to rule justly and make reforms. However Æthelred died in April 1016 in London, which was then under threat from Sweyn's son, King Canute (or Cnut) of Denmark. Æthelred was buried in the old St. Paul's Cathedral in London, but his tomb and monument were later destroyed in the Great Fire of London (1666).

His nickname is a corruption of the Old English 'unreed' (or 'unræd'), meaning badly counselled or poorly advised.

House of Denmark

Intermittently from 1013 to 1042

England became part of the Scandinavian empire under Danish kings from 1016 to 1042, following an earlier brief period from December 1013 to February 1014 under King Sweyn Forkbeard. At the height of its powers between 1028 and 1030, the House of Denmark – or in Danish, the House of Knýtlinga ('House of Cnut's Descendants') – ruled over Denmark, England and Norway.

England had been ravaged by the Danes every year from 997 to 1001, leading to the Wessex King Æthelred II ordering all Danish men to be slain. In the ensuing St. Brice's Day massacre of 1002 at Oxford, King Sweyn I of Denmark's sister was believed to have been killed. In revenge, Sweyn first invaded England in 1003 and by 1013 had overthrown Æthelred. He ruled only a few weeks, but his son Canute invaded soon after and established the House of Denmark in England. Canute had married Æthelred's widow, Emma of Normandy (they had a son, Harefoot) while still recognising his first wife, Ælfgifu of Northampton (they had a son Harthacnut) – each son went on to become King of England after Canute.

THE DANISH KINGS OF ENGLAND:

1013–1014

King Sweyn Forkbeard (1013–14)

1016–1042 *(restored)*

King Canute (Cnut the Great) (1016–35)

King Harold I, 'Harefoot' (1035–40)

King Harthacnut (1040–42)

KING SWEYN FORKBEARD

b. circa 960, d. 3 February 1014

REIGNED 1013–14

S**WEYN FORKBEARD** of Denmark invaded England in 1013, causing King Æthelred II the Unready to give up his kingship and flee to Normandy at the end of the year. King Sweyn was pronounced King of England on Christmas Day 1013.

King of Denmark since c. 985–87, Sweyn had been involved in sporadic raids on England alongside the Norwegians. The attacks on England intensified after the St. Brice's Day massacre of 1002 when Sweyn's sister was said to have been murdered. In 1013, Sweyn and his son Canute invaded through the Humber and the Trent, moving south. A Viking chief helped hold out London for Æthelred but finally succumbed to Sweyn, after which Æthelred fled the country.

After a few weeks of controlling his new English kingdom, Sweyn died on 3 February 1014. His son Canute was too inexperienced to do other than withdraw to Denmark. This left the way open for Æthelred to return, after being recalled by the English.

The descendants of Sweyn continue to reign in Denmark today. One of them, Margaret of Denmark, married James III of Scotland in 1469, introducing Sweyn's bloodline into the Scottish royal house.

Sweyn Forkbeard made what is now the Old Hall in Gainsborough the centre of his operations, but ruled for just 41 days.

King Edmund II (Ironside)

b. circa 990–93, d. 30 November 1016

Reigned 1016

EDMUND II succeeded to the throne on 23 April 1016 following the death of his father, King Æthelred II the Unready. Then in his twenties, Edmund had unexpectedly found himself heir after his two elder brothers both died by 1014. He inherited the war with the Danes from his father's reign and commanded the forces resisting King Canute.

While defending London, its citizens chose Edmund as king while the Witan (a council of high-ranking nobles and religious leaders) elected Canute. Suffering varying fortunes – during which time Edmund's brilliant performance earned him the nickname 'Ironside' – the battles ended in Edmund's defeat in October 1016 at the Battle of Assandun in Essex. Nevertheless, Canute agreed to partition the kingdom, leaving Wessex in the south for Edmund and the rest of the country north of the Thames for himself.

However, Edmund himself died the following month on 30 November (possibly assassinated) and Canute was accepted as king throughout England. Edmund was buried at Glastonbury Abbey. Edmund's children went into exile in Hungary, although his grandson Edgar the Ætheling was briefly pronounced king immediately after the Battle of Hastings (1066).

'… who was yclept (i.e. called)
"Ironside" for his bravery.'

ANGLO-SAXON CHRONICLE

King Canute (Cnut the Great)

b. circa 995, d. 12 November 1035

Reigned 1016–35

CANUTE won the English throne on the death of Edmund Ironside (r. 1016). Following centuries of Viking incursion, the Danes had finally crowned a King of England. Canute also became King of Denmark from 1018 and King of Norway from 1028, creating a North Sea Empire.

The son of Sweyn Forkbeard (r. 1013–14), Canute had accompanied his father into battles against King Æthelred II the Unready. For almost 20 years the Danish king brought a period of peace and prosperity to England, finding favour with his subjects for ruling well. Canute promised to rule by the laws of King Edgar the Peaceful (r. 959–75), recognising the rights of the Church and secular law. Canute's Christian marriage in 1017 to Emma of Normandy, widow of Æthelred II, was politically astute and followed an existing marriage to Ælfgifu of Northampton.

The famous legend of Canute failing to order the tide not to come in was not due to delusion about his own powers, but to demonstrate to his subjects that as a king he was not God.

Canute was succeeded by his son Harold Harefoot, son of Ælfgifu of Northampton.

'I bid the waves retreat but they pay no attention to me. I am not a fool.'

King Harold I, 'Harefoot'

b. circa 1015–17, d. 17 March 1040

Reigned 1035–40

HAROLD, as son of his father King Canute's first wife, Ælfgifu, claimed the English throne on the death of his father in opposition to his half-brother Harthacnut, son of Canute's second wife, Emma. As the sons were still young, it is suspected that in reality they were pawns of their formidable mothers and a compromise may have been reached: Harold was to rule as regent over a part of England while Harthacnut, regarded as the rightful heir, remained away fighting in Denmark. Nevertheless, by 1037 Harold – known as 'Harefoot' due to his speed and skill as a hunter – had established himself as king of the whole realm.

However, Harold died in Oxford in 1040 just five years into his reign, while Harthacnut was preparing to invade England to claim his throne. Thus a peaceful succession to Harthacnut occurred by accident.

King Harold I was buried in London, but Harthacnut is said to have had his body dug up, beheaded and thrown into the River Thames and nearby fens. His boby parts were gathered soon after and then reburied with due honour in the churchyard at St. Clement Danes in London.

'He went astray from the qualities and conduct of his father King Cnut, for he cared not at all … for courtesy, or for honour, but only for his own will.'

ANGLO-NORMAN CHRONICLE

King Harthacnut

b. circa 1018, d. 8 June 1042

Reigned 1040–42

HARTHACNUT, the son of King Canute's second wife Emma, acquired the throne bloodlessly on the death of his half-brother Harold Harefoot (r. 1035–40). At the time of his death, Harthacnut was sailing back to England with a fleet of warships intending to snatch back the throne. Harthacnut, also called Canute III, had been in Denmark where he was king from 1035 to 1042, though he failed to hold on to his father's throne in Norway.

Damningly, the Anglo-Saxon Chronicle recorded that Harthacnut 'never did anything worthy of a king while he reigned'. Only two years into his reign, aged around 23, Harthacnut died while attending a wedding feast. He was said to have been toasting the bride when he suddenly fell to the ground in a convulsion. He was the last Danish king to rule over England. His bones are thought to be held in a mortuary casket in Winchester Cathedral.

Significantly, a year before he died, Harthacnut had invited back to England from exile in Normandy his other half-brother Edward, Emma's son from her first marriage to Æthelred II the Unready.

He 'did nothing worthy of a king as long as he ruled'.

ANGLO-SAXON CHRONICLE

KING EDWARD THE CONFESSOR

b. circa 1001–05, d. 4 or 5 January 1066

REIGNED 1042–66

EDWARD was the son of Æthelred II the Unready and his second wife Emma (daughter of Richard I, Count of Normandy). Due to his family line and having been recalled from exile by his half-brother King Harthacnut (r. 1040–42), Edward was well-placed to press his claim to the throne when Harthacnut died, despite other contenders. Edward's succession restored the House of Wessex for the second time.

Sometimes portrayed as a pious nincompoop, others give him credit for holding the kingdom together. In 1045 Edward married Edith, daughter of the Earl of Godwin of Wessex. Having fallen out with the Godwin family, Edward apparently promised the throne to William, Duke of Normandy (his mother's great-nephew). However, things were patched up and Godwin's son Harold became a key adviser to King Edward. Attacks from Wales were successfully defended during this period.

Edward oversaw the rebuilding of Westminster Abbey, consecrated in December 1065, but died childless several days later in January 1066. With no obvious successor, a power struggle began for the throne. In 1161 Edward was canonised and the byname 'the Confessor' persisted to indicate one who suffered for his faith.

'Pleasant, but always dignified, he walked with eyes downcast, most graciously affable to one and all.'

HISTORICAL MANUSCRIPT

KING HAROLD II

b. circa 1020–23, d. 14 October 1066

REIGNED 1066

HAROLD Godwinson is said to have been chosen as successor by his childless brother-in-law, King Edward the Confessor (r. 1042–66), before his death. However, Edward is reputed to have visited a distant cousin, William, Duke of Normandy, in 1051 and promised him the throne at a time when Edward had fallen out with Harold's family. It is also said that Harold himself visited William in 1064 and swore an oath to support William's claim to the throne.

Despite the counterclaims, and with the support of the Witan (a council of high-ranking nobles and religious leaders), Harold was crowned at Westminster Abbey on 6 January 1066, shortly after Edward died on 4/5 January. In the Battle of Stamford Bridge on 25 September, Harold successfully repelled an invasion of Northumbria by the King of Norway, Harald Hardrada. Only days later Harold and his troops then famously rushed back south to defend an invasion by William, Duke of Normandy to claim the throne sworn to him by Harold. In the ensuing Battle of Hastings, Harold was killed on 14 October 1066, according to legend with an arrow shot through his eye.

Harold II, the last House of Wessex king, is also often cited as the last of the Anglo-Saxon kings before the Norman Conquest – despite Harold's Norse surname and his parents' links to Scandinavia.

'Seven feet of English ground, or as much more as he may be taller than other men.'

WHEN ASKED HOW MUCH OF ENGLAND HE WOULD GIVE UP

House of Normandy
1066–1154

Spanning England and France, this royal house ruled England from the Norman Conquest by William I in 1066 until the death of King Stephen in 1154, when the House of Plantagenet came to power with Henry II.

William's claim to the throne lay in a promise of succession by his distant English relative, King Edward the Confessor (r. 1042–66), who died childless. Additionally, William's wife Matilda was descended from King Alfred the Great. However, on Edward's death, William had to fight another claimant, Harold (Edward's brother-in-law), at the Battle of Hastings (1066) to secure the throne.

William the Conqueror's heirs ruled England until 1135, after which the throne was disputed between his grandchildren Matilda and Stephen. In addition to the King of England title, rulers from this house included Counts of Rouen and Dukes of Normandy.

During the rule of the House of Normandy, England is said to have borne the traits of a conquered country, administered by kings whose political and personal interests lay in France.

The Norman monarchs of England:

William I (William the Conqueror) (1066–87)

William II, 'Rufus' (1087–1100)

Henry I (1100–35)

Stephen (1135–54)

King William I (The Conqueror)

b. circa 1027–28, d. 9 September 1087

Reigned 1066–87

WILLIAM, Duke of Normandy, was crowned King of England on Christmas Day after defeating King Harold II at the Battle of Hastings in 1066. The illegitimate son of the previous Duke of Normandy, he set about cementing his claim by putting down Saxon revolts in the south-west as well as in the northern counties, resulting in the 'Harrying of the North'.

A powerful personality, William oversaw the start of work on the Tower of London in 1078 and ordered a survey of England in 1085, with the information being recorded in the famous Domesday Book, completed the following year. This gave him information about his new kingdom and the taxes he could raise.

After 1072, he visited England infrequently and was preoccupied with enemies in northern France. The famous Bayeux Tapestry was completed around 1077, depicting the Battle of Hastings entirely from a Norman perspective.

William died in 1087 from injuries after falling off his horse while besieging Nantes and on his deathbed divided his lands between his two sons. Unfortunately, during his royal send-off in France, his sarcophagus was found to be too small, leading to an unceremonious squeezing of his body into it.

'See – I have taken England with both my hands.'

REMARK AFTER HE STEPPED OFF HIS SHIP ON THE COAST OF ENGLAND AND FELL INTO THE SAND

King William II, 'Rufus'

b. 1056–60, d. 2 August 1100

Reigned 1087–1100

WILLIAM II, the third son (second surviving) of William I, inherited England after the death of his father during battle in France. William II immediately faced revolts in support of his elder brother Robert, who had inherited Normandy. Seeing off these revolts, William II ended up ruling Normandy himself, while his brother Robert went off to take part in the First Crusade.

William II finally defeated Malcolm III of Scotland in the Battle of Alnwick in 1093 and suppressed revolts in Northumbria in 1095 and a Welsh rebellion in 1098.

A blustering and inflammatory personality, combined with claims of extravagance and cruelty, meant William II was not a popular king. He was killed in 1100 while hunting in the New Forest, Hampshire, either by an accidental stray arrow or, controversially, on the orders of his younger brother Henry. Buried in Winchester Cathedral, the spot where he fell is marked to this day with the 'Rufus Stone'. Never married, William II died childless, which pointed to his younger brother's ascendancy.

William II's nickname 'Rufus' started appearing from the early twelfth century, referring to his red hair or ruddy complexion.

Here stood the oak tree, on which an arrow shot by Sir Walter Tyrrell at a stag, glanced and struck King William the Second … of which he instantly died …

RUFUS STONE INSCRIPTION

KING HENRY I

b. circa 1068–69, d. circa 1 or 2 December 1135

REIGNED 1100–35

HENRY I, William the Conqueror's fourth and youngest son, succeeded his older brother, William II (r. 1087–1100). However, the succession dispute with the eldest brother Robert continued; eventually the Treaty of Alton was signed in 1101, which confirmed Henry as king and Robert as Duke of Normandy.

Henry established an effective bureaucracy and extended a justice system. He became popular with the Saxons and married a Saxon princess, Edith (known as Matilda after marriage), daughter of Malcolm III of Scotland, forging a useful dynastic link. Still Robert continued his claim, but was imprisoned in Cardiff Castle in 1106, after which Henry ruled both England and Normandy for the rest of his life.

Fathering at least 21 illegitimate children, Henry's legitimate son and heir was drowned at sea in 1120, so Henry persuaded the powers to accept his daughter Matilda as successor. She was married to the powerful Count Geoffrey Plantagenet of Anjou in 1128. However, when Henry I died of food poisoning in 1135, his nephew (and grandson of William I) Stephen facilitated a coup and was offered the throne by the Council, who also declared a woman unfit to rule.

Henry's body was buried in England, but his entrails were said to have been removed and buried in Rouen, France.

'He preferred to contend by council rather than by the sword.'

William of Malmesbury

King Stephen

b. circa 1096–97, d. 25 October 1154

Reigned 1135–54

STEPHEN, son of William the Conqueror's daughter Adela, usurped the throne from his cousin Matilda, Henry I's daughter, despite being brought up and enriched in the court of his uncle Henry I (r. 1100–35).

Stephen spent the beginning of his reign in a civil war known as 'the Anarchy'. He was defeated by Owain Gwynedd of Wales in 1136 and raided constantly by the Scots. He also had to deal with invasion by Matilda in 1139, whose forces succeeded in capturing Stephen in the Battle of Lincoln in 1141, after which Matilda was proclaimed queen, supported by Earl Robert, Henry I's illegitimate son. Stephen's freedom was secured a year later in a swap for Earl Robert.

In 1148 Matilda abandoned her claim, but her son Henry Plantagenet invaded England and gathered support for a war against Stephen. The papacy sided with Henry's cause as a direct descendant of Henry I. Hastened by the sudden death of his own son Eustace, Stephen reached agreement with Henry in 1153 in the Treaty of Wallingford to recognise Henry as heir (passing over William, Stephen's second son).

Stephen died the following year and was buried at Faversham Abbey with his wife and son Eustace. Henry's succession followed peacefully in October 1154 after Stephen's death.

'... he was a mild man, and soft, and good, and no justice executed.'

English chronicler

House of Plantagenet
1154–1485

The English branch of this royal house reigned from 1154 to 1485 and includes two cadet branches: the House of Lancaster (see page 84) and the House of York (see page 92). This royal line began with those descended from the union between Geoffrey Plantagenet, Count of Anjou (father of Henry II) and his wife Matilda (daughter of Henry I).

The name Plantagenet is said to have derived from a nickname for Count Geoffrey, who often wore a sprig of the flowering shrub broom in his hat ('planta genista', Latin for 'plant broom').

FOURTEEN KINGS OF ENGLAND ORIGINATED FROM THE HOUSE OF PLANTAGENET (INCLUDING SIX FROM THE LANCASTER AND YORK BRANCHES):

King Henry II (1154–89)

King Richard I (Richard the Lionheart) (1189–99)

King John (1199–1216)

King Henry III (1216–72)

King Edward I, 'Longshanks' (1272–1307)

King Edward II (1307–27)

King Edward III (1327–77)

King Richard II (1377–99)

House of Lancaster

King Henry IV (1399–1413)

King Henry V (1413–22)

King Henry VI (1422–61 and 1470–71)

House of York

King Edward IV (1461–70 and 1471–83)

King Edward V (1483)

King Richard III (1483–85)

King Henry II

b. 5 March 1133, d. 6 July 1189

Reigned 1154–89

HENRY became the first Plantagenet King of England aged 21, succeeding his cousin Stephen (r. 1135–54). In 1162 Henry appointed Thomas Becket as Archbishop of Canterbury. However, they fell out in 1164 when Becket, following the Pope's views, refused to sign the Constitutions of Clarendon introduced by Henry to place limitations on the Church's jurisdiction over crimes committed by the clergy. In 1166 trial by jury was established for the first time, laying the foundations of English common law.

In 1170, Becket published papal letters voiding Henry's Clarendon Constitutions and was killed later that year in Canterbury Cathedral by four of Henry's knights. Meanwhile Henry had been showing support to Ireland's beleaguered King of Leinster and in 1171 invaded Ireland to be accepted as Lord of Ireland, thereby beginning its English settlement.

Regarded as a strong and able king, defending his vast Angevin empire both sides of the Channel, his wife Eleanor of Aquitaine (m. 1152) and his sons turned against Henry in a quest for land and power. Henry died in Anjou in 1189 and was buried in France.

Addicted to hunting and hawking, Henry was in his horse saddle so often he became bow-legged.

'What miserable drones and traitors have I nourished and promoted in my household, who let their lord be treated with such shameful contempt by a low-born clerk!'

King Richard I (The Lionheart)

b. 8 September 1157, d. 6 April 1199

Reigned 1189–99

RICHARD, the third son of Henry II (r. 1154–89), succeeded to the throne on the death of his father. Richard led the Third Crusade and won victories against Saladin, but narrowly failed to recover Jerusalem. While returning to England, he was held prisoner by Duke Leopold V of Austria, but released to the emperor Henry VI on payment of a large ransom. He returned briefly to England where his brother John had been ruling in his stead, but while also plotting against him – a scenario depicted in numerous Robin Hood films and stories.

Richard I died in 1199 from an infected crossbow wound, said to be the result of a lucky shot over a castle wall by a young boy during the siege of the castle of Châlus. Richard's heart was buried in Rouen, his entrails in Châlus, and the rest of his body beside his father.

Richard I is a national English hero whose massive bronze statue has long sat in Westminster Palace Yard. Although he acquired his legendary epithet 'Lionheart' due to his reputation as a warrior and crusader, he was also famed as a patron of troubadour poetry. Despite holding a special place in English hearts and legend, Richard in fact only spent about six month of his reign in England and spoke no English.

'The Lion by the Ant was slain.'

LATER REFERENCE TO RICHARD THE LIONHEART'S ASSASSINATION BY A BOY

King John

b. 24 December 1166, d. 18 or 19 October 1216

Reigned 1199–1216

JOHN LACKLAND succeeded to the throne on the death of his brother Richard I (r. 1189–99). In reality though, he had been acting as king for much of Richard's reign due to his absence in the Third Crusade.

By 1205 John had lost Normandy to Philip II of France, along with most other French lands. John tried to limit papal rights in clerical elections and Pope Innocent III was provoked into excommunicating England in 1209 (with the dispute not settled until 1213).

Aiming to raise funds to regain lost French lands, John's perceived repressive policies and excessive tax brought him into conflict with his barons and John was forced into signing the Magna Carta in 1215. His later rejection of it led to the First Barons' War (1215–17), during which John died of a fever at Newark. He was buried in Worcester Cathedral.

John's bad reputation as an evil tyrant has undergone modern re-examination, with some claiming him to have been the victim of subjective monastic records from the time and then later moralistic Victorian historians.

King John is said to have been the first European king to own a 'king's over-shirt for rising in the night' – more commonly known as a dressing gown.

'... one of the worst kings ever to rule England.'

Historian J. Gillingham (2001)

King Henry III

b. 1 October 1207, d. 16 November 1272

Reigned 1216–72

HENRY, son of King John (r. 1199–1216), was crowned king aged nine, with government in the hands of two regents until Henry assumed full power in 1227. Henry married Eleanor of Provence in 1236, with whom he had five children, including the future King Edward I.

Henry's accrual of financial debts to the papacy and his failed attempts to regain lost French territories led to a revolt against him in 1258 by the English barons. In response to their grievances, Henry agreed to limit his power under the Provisions of Oxford. However, when he repudiated them, the Second Barons' War broke out (1264–67), led by Simon de Montfort who was married to Henry's sister, Eleanor.

Henry was forced to call the first fledgling English Parliament at Westminster in 1265. Defeated at Lewes, Sussex, and imprisoned, Henry was restored in 1265 after defeating de Montfort at the Battle of Evesham. Henry died in 1272 at the Palace of Westminster and was buried in Westminster Abbey.

Noted for his love of art and learning, Henry had Westminster Abbey lavishly rebuilt from 1245 in a gothic style. He is also said to have kept a polar bear in the Tower of London, which he had taken to the River Thames each day to swim and fish.

'The most obsessive patron of art and architecture ever to have occupied the throne of England.'

ARCHITECTURAL HISTORIAN J. GOODALL (2011)

KING EDWARD I, 'LONGSHANKS'

b. 17 June 1239, d. 7 July 1307

REIGNED 1272–1307

EDWARD acceded to the throne an experienced statesman and soldier, having led his father Henry III's (r. 1216–72) forces against de Montfort. By 1284 he had established rule over Wales. Edward is best known as the 'Hammer of the Scots' after he defeated them at the Battle of Falkirk in 1298, although Robert the Bruce went on to be crowned King of Scotland in 1306. Edward brought back the contested Coronation Stone of Scone from Scotland to Westminster.

In 1290, a grieving Edward famously accompanied his deceased wife Eleanor of Castile's body back to London from Nottinghamshire. Twelve stone monuments, the 'Eleanor Crosses', were erected at Edward's overnight stops on the journey, including at Waltham Cross and Charing Cross.

During Edward's reign, Parliament came closer to its modern form in his summoning of the Model Parliament in 1295. Trying to invade Scotland again, Edward died in 1307 on his way north.

Nicknamed 'Longshanks' due to his long legs or shins, Edward is credited with ordering the construction of the 'Warwolf'. Sight of this gigantic catapult, suspected to be the largest in history, was enough to compel his opponents to surrender.

Here is Edward I,
Hammer of the Scots, 1308.
Keep the Vow.

From his tomb at Westminster Abbey

EDWARD, who was born at Caernarvon Castle, was created the first Prince of Wales in 1301 by his father Edward I (r. 1272–1307). He inherited a legacy of debt and unfinished war. In 1314 Edward was defeated in the Battle of Bannockburn, with the victory by Robert Bruce assuring later Scottish independence.

Edward was deposed in 1327 by his wife, Isabella of France, with her lover Roger de Mortimer and Parliament installed his son Edward III as king. Edward II was held captive and then murdered at Berkeley Castle in Gloucestershire, according to legend by having a red-hot poker thrust in his anus. There were other unlikely accounts that he in fact escaped to live as a hermit in Italy.

Edward is considered to be a weak and ineffectual king, too much under the influence of his favourites, many of whom the court took to exiling. Nevertheless, his son Edward III had a beautiful tomb erected for his father in Gloucester Cathedral, where a grand funeral took place.

Said to be in force to this day, Edward II introduced a statute in 1313 forbidding the wearing of armour in Parliament.

'… he has no high aims, no policy beyond the cunning of unscrupulous selfishness.'

HISTORIAN W. STUBBS (1875)

KING EDWARD III

b. 13 November 1312, d. 21 June 1377

REIGNED 1327–77

EDWARD was thrust to the throne aged 14 by Parliament, after his mother Isabella and her lover, Roger de Mortimer, led the formal deposing of his father Edward II (r. 1307–27). In 1330, aged 17, Edward III assumed full power and led a coup against the pair, having Roger de Mortimer executed and imprisoning his mother.

Edward continued battles to conquer Scotland and France. He defeated the Scottish at Halidon Hill in 1333. In 1337 he laid claim to the French throne through his mother, daughter of Philip IV of France, so beginning what became the Hundred Years War. English victories in France included the Battle of Crécy in 1346 and the capture of Calais in 1347.

Bubonic plague swept across England from 1348 to 1350, killing one-third of England's population and leaving shortages in labour for agriculture and the army. In 1370, Edward's eldest son, the 'Black Prince', raided Limoges massacring 3,000 people and fighting took place in Poitou, Brittany and La Rochelle. This brutality, along with his black armour and shield, earned him his name. While king and son were away fighting the costly war, another son, John of Gaunt, acted as head of government.

Edward III died aged 64 at Sheen Palace in Surrey.

'Honi soit qui mal y pense' – the original Middle French meaning 'Evil (or shame) be to him that evil thinks'.

TO THIS DAY FOUND ON THE BRITISH COAT OF ARMS AND BRITISH PASSPORTS

KING RICHARD II

b. 6 January 1367, d. 14 February 1400

REIGNED 1377–99

RICHARD was a grandson of Edward III (r. 1327–77) and son of the 'Black Prince' (Edward III's eldest son, d. 1376). Richard II came to the throne aged only ten, with government in the hands of a regency dominated by two of his uncles. Richard took control of the government in 1389. By this time an infamous Poll Tax had been levied which led to the 1381 Peasants' Revolt and Wat Tyler's march on London. Richard is said to have witnessed the slaying of Wat Tyler and stopped further escalation, though his later actions deepened the crisis.

In 1396, Richard married Isabella, daughter of the French King Charles VI and signed a 28-year truce with France. A year later Richard had some political opponents murdered or exiled, ensuring his absolute rule. In 1399 the exiled Henry Bolingbroke (Richard's cousin and later Henry IV) returned and seized the throne with relative ease while Richard was away fighting in Ireland. When he returned, Richard was imprisoned in Pontefract Castle and agreed to abdicate. However, he only survived his deposition by a year and died in 1400.

It is said that to celebrate Richard II's coronation in 1377, fountains of wine were opened across London.

'I will be your captain … Come with me into the fields and you shall have all you ask.'

TO WAT TYLER'S FOLLOWERS

PLANTAGENET: HOUSE OF LANCASTER BRANCH
1399–1461 and 1470–71

The House of Lancaster, symbolised by a red rose, is a branch of the royal house of the Plantagenets. The three kings from this house were descended from John of Gaunt, Duke of Lancaster (d. 1399).

The house was created originally in 1267 when Henry III (r. 1216–72) bestowed the earldom of Lancaster to his second son, Edmund (1245–96). The title was passed down to Edmund's sons, eventually falling to Blanche, Edmund's granddaughter, and her husband, John of Gaunt, third son of the Plantagenet King Edward III (r. 1327–77).

John of Gaunt's son, Henry IV established the royal dynasty of Lancaster in 1399 after deposing Richard II (r. 1377–99). In doing so, Henry created one of the warring factions in the Wars of the Roses which saw a dynastic power struggle between Edward III's descendants. The male line of the Lancaster house ended with the murder of Henry VI in 1471 in the Tower of London (following a period in captivity from 1461) and the triumph of the House of York through Edward IV, though the Lancastrian claim was taken up by Henry Tudor (the future King Henry VII).

House of Lancaster kings:

King Henry IV (1399–1413)

King Henry V (1413–22)

King Henry VI (1422–61 and 1470–71)

King Henry IV

b. 15 April 1366 or 1367, d. 20 March 1413

Reigned 1399–1413

HENRY BOLINGBROKE, grandson of Edward III (r. 1327–77) and the eldest son of John of Gaunt, Duke of Lancaster, laid claim to the throne after deposing his cousin Richard II (r. 1377–99). Within the House of Plantagenet, Henry was the first king of the House of Lancaster branch and the first since the Norman Conquest to be a native English speaker.

Much of Henry IV's 13-year reign was spent trying to control Parliament and the clergy. Henry had to retain the support of the Church by agreeing to a law for the burning of heretics. He also had to deal with an uprising in Wales in 1400 by Owen Glendower, who had declared himself Prince of Wales.

Taking a toll on his health, Henry suffered either a series of strokes or a leprosy-like illness that left him mostly incapacitated by 1410. He died weak and exhausted at Westminster Abbey in 1413 aged 45 or 46, and was buried in Canterbury Cathedral. Despite rebellions by the Percy family from Northumberland, there was no serious threat to accession by his son, the future Henry V.

Henry's reign also saw the death of the poet Geoffrey Chaucer in 1400, leaving The Canterbury Tales unfinished.

The new king ruled 'not so much by title of blood as by popular election'.

FIFTEENTH-CENTURY WRITER

King Henry V

b. 9 August or 16 September 1386 or 1387,
d. 31 August 1422

Reigned 1413–22

HENRY V succeeded his father Henry IV in 1413 in his mid-twenties and subsequently pursued the claim of his great-grandfather, Edward III (r. 1327–77), to the French crown. He continued the Hundred Years War by invading Normandy in 1415 and then famously defeating the French at Agincourt: 6,000 Frenchmen were killed while fewer than 400 English soldiers died.

His military victories over the French led to the Treaty of Troyes in 1420, giving him control of the French government. In the same year Henry V married Catherine of Valois, daughter of the French King Charles VI, gaining recognition as heir to the French throne. However, Henry was to die several weeks before his father-in-law, leaving Henry's baby son (the future Henry VI) as King of France and England.

The start of Henry's reign fired widespread enthusiasm and symbolised a welcome break from the gloomier recent past. Henry encouraged the keeping of festivals and the use of English in government.

Henry died from dysentery in 1422 aged 35 or 36, and was buried in Westminster Abbey. He had ruled for just over nine years: the shortest reign of any of England's eight King Henrys.

'In his youth he had been wild and reckless … but as soon as he was crowned suddenly he was changed into a new man.'

Fifteenth-century chronicler, Thomas Walsingham

King Henry VI

b. 6 December 1421, d. 21 May 1471

Reigned 1422–61 and 1470–71

HENRY inherited both the English and French crowns, aged 8–9 months, on the death of his father Henry V and his grandfather French King Charles VI. Regents ruled until Henry was crowned King of England in 1429 and King of France in 1431; he assumed full power in England by the early 1440s.

Henry sided with those opposed to continuing the Hundred Years War with France. In 1445 he married the indomitable Margaret of Anjou. French losses and the unpopularity of the government, together with Henry's growing mental illness, led to Richard Plantagenet staking his claim to the throne. The Wars of the Roses (1455–85) pitted the King's Lancastrian forces against the Yorkists. Richard was killed in 1460, with his son proclaiming himself king as Edward IV in 1461. Henry was captured, but temporarily restored in 1470. Months later, in 1471, he was imprisoned in the Tower of London and stabbed to death.

Henry VI was the youngest ever king to accede to the English throne, the only English king ever to be crowned King of France and the only one to have inherited the two kingdoms and lost both.

During Henry VI's reign, Joan of Arc was convicted of heresy before being burnt at the stake in 1431 and the Gutenberg Bible was completed around 1455.

'… a mild spoken, pious king, but half-witted in affairs of state.'

Bishop of St Albans

PLANTAGENET: HOUSE OF YORK BRANCH
1461–70 and 1471–85

The House of York, symbolised by a white rose, is a branch of the royal house of Plantagenet. The York dynasty was first established when Edward III (r. 1327–77) made his fourth son, Edmund, Duke of York in 1362. The Duke of York title in turn passed down to Edmund's grandson, Richard Plantagenet, whose two sons – Edward IV and Richard III – each eventually went on to rule. The Yorkist claim to the throne lay in descent from a fourth son of Edward III, while the claim of the reigning monarch, Henry VI of the rival House of Lancaster, descended from a third son of Edward III.

These counterclaims were fought out in the Wars of the Roses (1455–85). Richard Plantagenet was killed in battle in 1460, but the following year his son became king, as Edward IV, when Henry VI was captured. Edward IV's son and brother each went on to be king. Henry VII's Lancastrian victory at Bosworth in 1485 and subsequent marriage to Elizabeth of York brought the two warring houses together, ending the Wars of the Roses.

House of York kings:

King Edward IV (1461–70 and 1471–83)

King Edward V (1483)

King Richard III (1483–85)

King Edward IV

b. 28 April 1442, d. 9 April 1483

Reigned 1461–70 and 1471–83

EDWARD'S House of York emerged victorious over Henry VI's House of Lancaster in the latest Wars of the Roses. After his father Richard Plantagenet's death, Edward was proclaimed king in 1461 in place of the captured Henry VI. This victory followed the bloody Battle of Towton, in which 28,000 soldiers were said to have been killed.

In 1464 Edward married Elizabeth Woodville, the widow of a commoner, which offended some supporters who then sided with the Lancastrians, now organised by the ailing Henry VI's spirited wife Margaret of Anjou.

Although Henry VI was restored briefly in 1470, Edward recovered the throne in 1471 by defeating the Lancastrians at the Battle of Tewkesbury. Henry VI was imprisoned and murdered in the same year.

Suspecting him of treason, Edward had his brother George, Duke of Clarence killed in 1478 at the Tower of London, reportedly by drowning in a butt of malmsey (fortified wine).

During Edward IV's reign, the first printing press was set up by William Caxton at Westminster in 1476 and the Spanish Inquisition tribunal was established in 1478. Edward died in his bed in 1483 after a short illness and was buried in St. George's Chapel at Windsor Castle.

Said to have restored law and order in England, Edward's royal motto was modus et ordo, or 'method and order'.

King Edward V

b. 2 or 4 November 1470, d. circa 1483

Reigned 1483

EDWARD, just 12 years old, succeeded to the throne on the death of his father, Edward IV. However, on his journey to London to be proclaimed king, Edward's attendants were arrested by his paternal uncle Richard of Gloucester claiming a conspiracy. Edward was thus separated from his mother and siblings. Edward was installed at apartments in the Tower of London to prepare for his coronation, joined there by his younger brother Richard of York. Gradually the princes were seen less frequently, until they were never seen again. Meanwhile, their uncle Richard declared the princes illegitimate later in 1483 and himself as the rightful heir to the crown and the future Richard III.

The princes were widely believed to have been murdered by their uncle. Much later, Sir Thomas More's writings claimed that the princes were buried 'at the stair-foot, meetly deep' and Shakespeare portrayed Richard III as an evil, murderous uncle. In 1674 two skeletons were found buried under a stone staircase during works to the Tower. The 1933 exhumation of these remains, reburied at Westminster Abbey, proved only they were human and approximately of the correct ages.

Edward V was the shortest lived monarch in English history and remained uncrowned.

Edward '… like a victim prepared for sacrifice, sought remission of his sins by daily confession and penance, because he believed that death was facing him'.

A VISITING DOCTOR

King Richard III

b. 2 October 1452, d. 22 August 1485

Reigned 1483–85

RICHARD, the brother of Edward IV and son of Richard Plantagenet, had distinguished himself in the Wars of the Roses. On Edward IV's death in 1483, Richard became protector to his nephew, the 12-year-old Edward V. However, in the same year, he declared Edward IV's two sons illegitimate, thereby securing the crown for himself.

Otherwise considered a capable ruler, he was dogged by suspicions that he had murdered his young nephews, Edward V and his brother Richard of York, when they disappeared. Some think his crimes were exaggerated by Tudor propaganda.

Richard's only son Edward died, aged nine, in 1484 and his wife Anne died a year later. In 1485, Henry Tudor, Earl of Richmond, raised a rebellion and gathered support for his Lancastrian claim to the Yorkist-held throne. Richard was defeated that year and killed by Tudor's army at Bosworth Field. With Henry's crowning that year, the Wars of the Roses and the Plantagenet dynasty came to an end.

Richard III's skeleton was discovered in 2012 in a Leicester car park and his bones reburied at Leicester Cathedral in 2015; analysis of his skull showed tooth decay and teeth grinding.

'I understand that you want my friendship in good form and manner, which contents me well enough; for I have no intention of breaking such truces.'

Letter sent to Louis XI of France, 18 August 1483

House of Tudor
1485–1603

The House of Tudor was established by Henry VII in 1485, bringing both the Wars of the Roses and the House of Plantagenet to an end. The Tudor dynasty was descended from the Welsh Owen Tudor (1400–61), second husband of Catherine of Valois (widow of Henry V of England). Their son Edmund married the great-granddaughter of John of Gaunt and was father of Henry VII, who became king by defeating Richard III at the Battle of Bosworth Field in 1485.

Henry VIII's break with the papacy in 1534 was a significant feature of this dynasty, marking the beginning of the Reformation and the establishment of the Anglican Church under Elizabeth I. Henry VIII's will, also an Act of Parliament (1544), stated that the descendants of his younger sister, Mary, should be crowned if Henry's own three children should die without an heir. After Elizabeth I's death without an heir, the Scottish King James VI (descendant of Henry's other sister, Margaret) succeeded to the English throne as James I.

The five Tudor monarchs of England:

Henry VII (Henry Tudor) (1485–1509)

Henry VIII (1509–47)

Edward VI (1547–53)

Mary I (1553–58)

Elizabeth I (1558–1603)

King Henry VII

b. 28 January 1457, d. 21 April 1509

Reigned 1485–1509

HENRY TUDOR, descendant of John of Gaunt, claimed the crown in 1485 after victory at the Battle of Bosworth Field against Richard III's Yorkist army. He was to be the last English monarch to seize power on the battlefield. His marriage in 1486 to Elizabeth of York united the warring Houses of Lancaster and York and gave rise to a new House of Tudor. The Tudor rose symbolised the union by representing the red rose of the Lancastrians superimposed upon the white rose of the Yorkists.

Henry invaded France in 1491 but agreed to retreat in return for a large amount of money, adding to the great private fortune which he amassed in his time.

Henry VII was the first English monarch to have a fully realised portrait stamped onto his coins.

In 1503 Henry VII's daughter Margaret married James IV of Scotland, thereby giving James' descendants a claim to the English throne. Henry VII died in 1509 at Richmond Palace aged 52, the same year that his second son, Prince Henry (the future King Henry VIII) married his elder brother's widow, Catherine of Aragon.

During Henry's reign, Christopher Columbus crossed the Atlantic in 1492 and founded the 'West Indies', believing that he has sailed around the world to India.

'... I give you to understand that no Christian heart can be more full of joy and gladness than the heart of me, your poor exiled friend.'

LETTER CIRCULATED AROUND NOVEMBER 1484

King Henry VIII

b. 28 June 1491, d. 28 January 1547

Reigned 1509–47

HENRY, the second son of Henry VII, only came to the throne because of his elder brother's death in 1502. In 1509 Henry married his brother's widow, Catherine of Aragon, daughter of the Spanish King.

Henry had an active foreign policy under the guidance of his Lord Chancellor, Cardinal Wolsey. Having failed to persuade the Pope to grant Henry a divorce, Wolsey was charged with treason and died in 1530 on his way to trial. Sir Thomas More had replaced him in 1529, but also fell foul of Henry and was executed in 1535. After cutting ties with Rome, Henry proclaimed himself head of the Church of England, dissolved monasteries and divorced Catherine.

Henry famously married six times in pursuit of a male heir. After his divorce from Catherine, Henry took the following wives: Anne Boleyn (m. 1533, executed 1536); Jane Seymour (m. 1536, died 1537); Anne of Cleves (m. 1540, annulled 1540); Catherine Howard (m. 1540, executed 1542); and Catherine Parr (m. 1543). This gave rise to the well-known mnenonic to remember their fates: 'Divorced, beheaded, died, divorced, beheaded, survived'.

Obese and suffering from long-term health issues, Henry died in 1547 and was buried in St. George's Chapel at Windsor Castle. Succeeded by his only son, Edward VI (born to Jane Seymour), both of Henry's daughters also went on to become monarchs (Mary, born to Catherine of Aragon, and Elizabeth, born to Anne Boleyn).

'You have sent me a Flanders mare!'

ON FIRST MEETING ANNE OF CLEVES,
ABOUT TO BECOME HIS FOURTH WIFE

King Edward VI

b. 12 October 1537, d. 6 July 1553

Reigned 1547–53

EDWARD, the only son of Henry VIII (r. 1509–47), came to the throne aged nine, although government was entrusted to his uncle Edward Seymour, Duke of Somerset (to be replaced later by John Dudley, Earl of Warwick). Edward became a staunch Protestant. Thomas Cranmer wrote the Book of Common Prayer in 1549 and the uniformity of worship helped turn England into a Protestant state. Meanwhile the 1549 First Act of Uniformity made the Roman Catholic Mass illegal and ordered the removal of icons and statues of the saints.

In 1553 aged 15, Edward VI died of tuberculosis at Greenwich Palace and was buried in Westminster Abbey. After his death there was a dispute over the succession. Edward named Lady Jane Grey (Protestant and his cousin once removed) as heir, excluding his half-sisters Mary (Catholic) and Elizabeth. However, after Edward's death the decision was disputed. Mary and her supporters had Lady Jane Grey arrested after only nine days' rule and Mary was crowned instead.

Despite his brief rule and his young age, Edward VI is credited with being the first English monarch to charter an exploration of the Arctic. This eventually led to a letter being delivered to Ivan the Terrible, initiating trade between England and Russia.

'I will say with certain intention, that I will see my laws strictly obeyed, and those who break them shall be watched and denounced.'

To his half-sister Mary I, who was ignoring his anti-Catholic laws (Greenwich, 1551)

Queen Mary I

b. 18 February 1516, d. 17 November 1558

Reigned 1553–58

MARY, the eldest child of Henry VIII, by Catherine of Aragon, was overlooked for succession when her brother Edward VI died in 1553 naming a cousin, the 15-year-old Protestant Lady Jane Grey, instead. After she had ruled only nine days, Mary and her supporters seized the crown from Grey with little difficulty and executed her in 1554. Mary earned the moniker 'Bloody Mary' for her persecution and many executions of Protestants.

Mary had her half-sister, Princess Elizabeth imprisoned in the Tower in 1554 on suspicion of being involved in the Protestant rebellions against her, releasing her a year later.

In 1554 Mary married Philip of Spain, heir to the Spanish throne. As a devout Catholic, Mary had Parliament re-establish Catholicism in England and restore papal authority. Persecution of Protestants began with burnings at the stake for heresy, including in 1556 Thomas Cranmer, former Archbishop of Canterbury.

When Mary's husband became King Philip II of Spain in 1556, he left England, never to return. He persuaded Mary to support Spain and declare war on France. As a result, England's last French possession, Calais, was lost to the French in 1558. Mary died that year at St. James's Palace, London and was buried in Westminster Abbey.

'She was a King's daughter;
she was a King's sister;
she was a King's wife.'

John White, Bishop of Winchester,
at Mary I's funeral

QUEEN ELIZABETH I

b. 7 September 1533, d. 24 March 1603

REIGNED 1558–1603

ELIZABETH, the second child of Henry VIII, by second wife Anne Boleyn, became queen on the death of her Catholic half-sister Mary. Elizabeth dealt with claims to the crown by Mary, Queen of Scots by imprisoning her in 1568 and executing her for treason in 1587.

Noted for her learning and wisdom, Elizabeth's long 44-year rule brought a welcome period of relative stability and prosperity to England. The 1559 Acts of Supremacy and Uniformity restored the Protestant Church in England, although in religion matters she was moderate and avoided persecution. The Spanish Armada was defeated in 1588, foiling an attempted invasion.

The Elizabethan age was expansionist in commerce and geographical exploration, forging a sense of English identity across the world. Raleigh famously brought back potatoes and tobacco from the New World in 1565 and by 1580 Francis Drake sailed around the world in the Golden Hind. Arts and literature also flourished: Shakespeare wrote many key plays and London's Globe Theatre was opened in 1599. The first slave-trading voyages were started in 1562 to America and the seeds of colonisation were sown with the founding of the East India Company in 1600.

Elizabeth never married, despite many suitors, and was the last of the five Tudor monarchs. She was buried in Westminster Abbey, alongside her half-sister Mary.

'I know I have the body but of a weak and feeble woman, but I have the heart and stomach of a king, and of a king of England too.'

AT TILBURY WAITING FOR THE SPANISH ARMADA, 1588

HOUSE OF STUART
1603–49 and 1660–1714

The Stuart (or 'Stewart') royal family inherited the Scottish throne in 1371 and the English throne in 1603, holding it until Queen Anne died in 1714 without heirs. The royal house was interrupted in 1649 by the establishment of Oliver Cromwell's Commonwealth, but was restored in 1660 with Charles II. The 1701 Act of Settlement under William III established Hanoverian and Protestant succession to the throne.

The Stuarts originated from Brittany before settling in Scotland at the invitation of King David I of Scotland, who gave one of them the title of royal steward. The title became heritable and the family became known as Stewart, until it was modified under French influence to Stuart.

The last male Stuarts of the British royal line were James II's son James Edward (d. 1766), known as the Old Pretender, and his sons Charles Edward (d. 1788), known as the Young Pretender and Bonnie Prince Charlie, and Henry (d. 1807), Cardinal Duke of York.

SIX ENGLISH MONARCHS
ORIGINATED FROM THIS HOUSE:

1603–1649

King James I (1603–25)

King Charles I (1625–49)

1660–1714 *(restored after the Commonwealth)*

King Charles II (1660–85)

King James II (1685–88)

King William III and Queen Mary II (1689–1702)

Queen Anne (1702–14)

KING JAMES I

b. 19 June 1566, d. 27 March 1625

REIGNED 1603–25

JAMES I was King of Scotland (as James VI) at the time he succeeded to the English throne following Elizabeth I's death without issue, thereby uniting England and Scotland. Although his mother Mary, Queen of Scots, had been executed by Elizabeth I's government in 1587, James had barely known her and his own Protestantism was at odds with her Catholicism.

James alienated the English with his High Church views and his attempts to build alliances with Spain. He created suspicion in Parliament, with his assertion of divine right going against the English political traditions of the Magna Carta and common law. His perceived generosity toward the Scottish annoyed many, leading to the English Parliament rejecting union with Scotland in 1607.

James, who suffered ill health in later years, died in 1625 and was buried in Westminster Abbey.

During James' reign, Guy Fawkes and other Catholic dissidents tried to blow up the King and Parliament in the infamous Gunpowder Plot of 1605, but they were betrayed and hung. In 1611, an English translation of the Bible was made at the order of James, known as the King James Bible, and became widely used. His rule also saw Shakespeare die in 1616 and the Pilgrim Fathers sail for America in the Mayflower, founding Plymouth in 1620.

James I kept an elephant in St James's Park – it is said to have been given a gallon of wine every winter morning.

'What God hath conjoined let no man separate. I am the husband and the whole isle is my lawful wife.'

ON THE UNION OF THE CROWNS OF SCOTLAND AND ENGLAND, 1603

KING CHARLES I

b. 19 November 1600, d.30 January 1649

REIGNED 1625–49

CHARLES I succeeded his father James I, as the eldest son had died of typhoid in 1612. A strong believer in divine right, Charles dissolved Parliament in 1629 and ruled without it until 1640. This was despite the Petition of Right having been accepted in 1428, recognising the rights of the subject.

Although Parliament was again summoned in 1640, continuing political clashes, including Charles' attempts to have some MPs arrested, led to the outbreak of the English Civil War in 1642. Charles' Royalist forces were eventually defeated by the New Model Army, led by Oliver Cromwell. Charles was imprisoned at Carisbrooke Castle and then tried for treason. Found guilty and condemned to death he was beheaded on 30 January 1649 in Whitehall. The monarchy was abolished and a republic, the Commonwealth of England, was declared which ruled by Parliament for the next 11 years under Cromwell, the Lord Protector from 1653 to 1658.

Charles I was the only king ever to be executed. His head was said to have been sewn back on his body before being buried in St. George's Chapel at Windsor Castle.

During Charles' reign development of a house and gardens began on the site of the future Buckingham Palace, land which had come into royal hands in 1536.

During Charles' reign, development of a house and gardens began on land in royal hands since 1536 – where Buckingham Palace stands today.

'I go from a corruptible to an incorruptible Crown.'

PRIOR TO HIS EXECUTION

Commonwealth
1649–60

For an 11-year period from 1649 to 1660, Britain had no monarch or royal house.

In January 1649 the reigning sovereign, Charles I from the House of Stuart, was tried for treason by a 'Rump Parliament' (a small remnant of the Commons following a purge) after failing to agree to constitutional concessions. Oliver Cromwell was one of 135 commissioners in the High Court of Justice who, when the King refused to plead, found him guilty of treason and condemned him to death: the King was beheaded on 30 January 1649.

The abolition of the monarchy and House of Lords followed on 19 May 1649, when England was declared a republic and the Commonwealth was set up. Executive authority lay in a Council of State with Cromwell as its chairman. By 1653, having dissolved the Rump Parliament by force, Cromwell became Lord Protector. Some view the Commonwealth period as one of military dictatorship, while others point to its foreign successes and religious tolerance.

When Cromwell died in September 1658, his third son Richard succeeded him as Lord Protector but proved ineffectual. Showing little zeal for continued republicanism, a new Council of State was established, Richard allowed to fade away and the monarchy restored on 29 May 1660.

Oliver Cromwell

b. 25 April 1599, d. 3 Sept 1658

***Oliver Cromwell**, born in Huntingdon and the son of a small landowner, was a descendant of the sister of Henry VIII's minister Thomas Cromwell. A puritan and intensely religious man, Cromwell entered the Parliament of 1628-29 and became prominent in events leading to the Civil War on the side of the Parliamentarians or 'Roundheads'. He organised and led the New Model Army to victory at Naseby in 1645 against the forces of King Charles I.*

Following the establishment of the Commonwealth, Cromwell commanded campaigns in Ireland and Scotland. He also supressed the leaders of the Levellers, who demanded radical reforms. In 1653 he expelled the Rump Parliament by force and was appointed Lord Protector for life – king in all but name.

One of the most controversial figures in British history, Cromwell refused an offer of the crown by Parliament in 1657. He died in 1658 aged 59 and his body was posthumously executed in 1661.

'I tell you we will cut off his head with the crown upon it.'

At the trial of Charles I, January 1649

King Charles II

b. 29 May 1630, d. 6 February 1685

Reigned 1660–85

CHARLES, the eldest son of Charles I, became King of England after the collapse of Cromwell's Commonwealth: a Rump (leftover) Parliament was revived and accepted the restoration of the monarchy. Much of Charles II's reign was spent at war with the Dutch, from whom 'New Amsterdam' was seized in America in 1664 and renamed 'New York'.

Parliament forced Charles to accept a Test Act in 1673 which kept Catholics out of political office. Following fabrication of a 'Popish plot', an Exclusion Bill in 1679 sought to exclude James, Charles's Catholic brother, from the succession. Having wanted to restore Catholicism in England, it was not until his death that Charles was received into the Catholic religion.

Known as the Merry Monarch, despite marrying Catherine of Braganza in 1662 and having no legitimate heir, the hedonistic Charles had a string of mistresses and some say as many as 14 illegitimate children. Under his rule, the Great Plague of London took hold in 1665, followed by the Great Fire in 1666, which destroyed much of London, and the new Habeas Corpus Act of 1679 forbade imprisonment without trial.

Over 500 English pubs are named 'The Royal Oak' to commemorate the tree in which Charles desperately hid from Cromwell's anti-monarchist forces in 1651, nine years before the Restoration.

'I always admired virtue –
but I could never imitate it.'

King James II

b. 14 October 1633, d. 16 September 1701

Reigned 1685–88

JAMES, the second son of Charles I (r. 1625–49), succeeded his brother Charles II. He had become a Catholic in 1671, leading to attempts to exclude him from succession. A failed rebellion in Scotland attempted to enthrone Charles II's illegitimate son, the Duke of Monmouth.

The oddity of a Catholic king as head of the Anglican state continued, though James pressed the Catholic case: he issued the Declaration of Indulgence to suspend all laws against Catholics and repealed the 1673 Test Act which kept Catholics out of office.

In 1688, his Catholic second wife gave birth to a son and Catholic heir (James Edward Stuart, the future Old Pretender), while the two daughters from his first marriage, Mary and Anne, were Protestant. Following concerns about James' attempts to control politics and religion, Whig and Tory leaders finally invited the Dutch Protestant William of Orange, husband of daughter Mary, to take the throne. This 1688 'Glorious Revolution' saw many English Protestants defecting to William, including James II's other daughter Anne.

James fled to France attempting an uprising in Ireland, but was defeated at the 1690 Battle of the Boyne and died in exile in France. James II fathered two future sovereigns, Mary and Anne.

'If occasion were, I hope God would give me his grace to suffer death for the true Catholic religion as well as banishment.'

Speaking about his exile from England after changing his religion

King William III and Queen Mary II

b. 4 November 1650, d. 8 March 1702

Reigned 1689–1702

WILLIAM OF ORANGE became joint sovereign with his wife, Mary II, the eldest daughter of the previous monarch, James II. William's mother was Mary Stuart, eldest daughter of Charles I (r. 1625–49), so by marrying a cousin William had a double claim to the throne.

Parliament passed the 1689 Bill of Rights laws stipulating that no Catholic could succeed to the throne and also limiting royal powers: significantly no monarch could withhold laws passed by Parliament.

William quashed Jacobite uprisings in support of James II at Dunkeld, Scotland in 1689 and defeated Catholic forces from France loyal to James in the 1690 Battle of the Boyne in Ireland. Catholics in Ireland were allowed to practise their religion under the 1691 Treaty of Limerick.

William continued to rule alone when Mary II died in 1694 and the 1701 Act of Settlement established Hanoverian and Protestant succession to the throne. William died in 1702 after a riding accident and was buried in Westminster Abbey alongside his wife.

William and Mary were the only official joint monarchs to have ruled Britain (although some consider Mary I and Phillip II to have also been joint rulers).

'The liberties of England and the Protestant religion I will maintain.'

ON LANDING IN ENGLAND TO TAKE THE CROWN FROM CATHOLIC JAMES II

QUEEN ANNE

b. 6 February 1665, d. 1 August 1714

REIGNED 1702–14

ANNE, successor to her sister's husband, William III, was crowned Queen of England and Ireland aged 37. She was the second daughter of James II (r. 1685–1688) by his Protestant first wife.

Anne had married Prince George of Denmark in 1683. In 1700, having suffered 18 miscarriages, her only surviving son became ill and died.

When Anne took the throne, England had just declared war on France as part of the War of the Spanish Succession. Under the Duke of Marlborough the English won a series of battles, notably the Battle of Blenheim in 1704, and exerted a new increased degree of influence over Europe. Britain captured Gibraltar from Spain the same year.

Notably, the 1707 Act of Union united England and Scotland and transferred the seat of Scottish government to London. In 1708, Anne's half-brother the Old Pretender, the Catholic son of James II, unsuccessfully attempted to gain the throne.

The War of the Spanish Succession was finally brought to an end by the Treaty of Utrecht signed by Britain and France in 1713. Anne died the following year at Kensington Palace and was buried in Westminster Abbey beside her husband and children.

During Anne's reign, St Paul's Cathedral in London was completed by Sir Christopher Wren.

'I can very sincerely assure you there is not anything you can expect or desire from me which I shall not be ready to do for the happiness and prosperity of England.'

ANNE'S FIRST SPEECH TO PARLIAMENT, MARCH 1702

HOUSE OF HANOVER
1714–1901

A German royal dynasty, this house ruled Great Britain and Ireland from George I in 1714 to the end of Victoria's reign in 1901.

With the aim of ensuring that the English crown continued to fall to Protestants rather than Catholics, the 1701 Act of Settlement passed succession to Hanover on the death of Queen Anne (House of Stuart) who died childless in 1714. After Anne the crown fell to Sophia, Electress of Hanover, as granddaughter of James I, and her descendants, thereby passing over many Catholics who would fall in the normal line of succession. As Sophia died just before Anne, the crown went to Sophia's son, George I.

From 1714 Hanover was part of the British crown up until 1837 when its laws barred Victoria as a woman from ruling the region. The Hanover succession passed instead to William IV's brother.

The House of Hanover ended with the start of Edward VII's reign in 1901, whose dynastic name was Saxe-Coburg-Gotha, via his father Prince Albert.

THE SIX MONARCHS FROM THE HOUSE OF HANOVER WERE:

George I (1714–27)

George II (1727–60)

George III (1760–1820)

George IV (1820–30)

William IV (1830–37)

Victoria (1837–1901)

King George I

b. 28 May 1660, d. 11 June 1727

Reigned 1714–27

GEORGE, the first King of Great Britain and the first from the House of Hanover, was great-grandson of James I (r. 1603–25), son of Sophia (James I's granddaughter) and a distant cousin of his predecessor Queen Anne. The Elector of Hanover since 1698, he arrived in England aged 54 speaking only a few words of English.

George favoured the Whig Party largely due to their mutual opposition to the Tory peace with France at Utrecht in 1713 under Anne. In 1721 the Whig Sir Robert Walpole was re-appointed First Lord of the Treasury, effectively establishing the role now commonly known as prime minister.

One of the most serious crises of George I's reign was the collapse of the South Sea Company in 1720, leaving its investors ruined. George spent most of his reign in Germany, never having learned much English, leaving his son (and future George II) as regent. He divorced his wife Sophia in 1694 and had her imprisoned for life. George I died in Hanover in 1727 aged 67.

George I allegedly declared all pigeon droppings to be the property of the crown because they contain saltpetre (potassium nitrate), which can be used to make gunpowder.

'My people,
I have come for all your goods.'

ARRIVING AT DOVER,
WITH A MISTRESS ON EACH ARM

King George II

b. 30 October 1683, d. 25 October 1760

Reigned 1727–60

GEORGE II, as only son, succeeded his father as King of Great Britain and Elector of Hanover. Sir Robert Walpole provided continuity and support in his role as prime minister until the Whigs fell in 1742.

Another Jacobite rebellion was attempted in 1745 when Bonnie Prince Charlie (grandson of the Catholic James II, r. 1685–88) tried to restore the Stuarts. He and the Scots were defeated brutally at Culloden in 1746 by the Duke of Cumberland, King George's youngest son.

George II's victory at Dettingen, Bavaria in 1743 in the War of the Austrian Succession was the last battle commanded by a British king, with the 1748 Treaty of Aix-la-Chapelle ending that war.

Britain declared war with France in 1756, beginning the Seven Years War. The following year, Robert Clive won the Battle of Plassey and secured the Indian province of Bengal for Britain. In 1759, British supremacy in Canada was established when James Wolfe captured Quebec from the French.

George died in 1760 aged 76 and became the most recent monarch to be buried in Westminster Abbey.

During George II's reign, botanical gardens were first laid at Kew and Britain adopted the Georgian calendar, whereby 1 January replaced 25 March as the first day of the year.

'I hate bainting, and boetry too! Neither the one nor the other ever did any good.'

King George III

b. 4 June 1738, d. 29 January 1820

Reigned 1760–1820

GEORGE, due to the death of his father Frederick in 1751, succeeded his grandfather George II. He was the first of the Hanoverian kings to be born in Great Britain.

His reign is marked by the loss of the American colonies, after the Boston Tea Party in 1773 led to the American War of Independence. On 4 July 1776, the American Congress passed the Declaration of Independence which Britain finally recognised in the 1783 Treaty of Paris. Elsewhere, Nelson's 1805 victory at the Battle of Trafalgar against the joint French and Spanish navies was followed by the defeat of Napoleon at the Battle of Waterloo in 1815.

The 1800 Act of Union with Ireland united the Parliaments of England and Ireland, giving rise to the new royal title of King of the United Kingdom of Great Britain and Ireland.

The latter part of George's reign was dominated by mental illness, possibly from the blood disease porphyria. When the King finally relapsed, a regency was established in 1811 under his eldest son, the future George IV. He died at Windsor Castle early in 1820 and was buried in St. George's Chapel.

During George III's reign, Captain James Cook landed in Australia in 1770.

'I desire what is good. Therefore, everyone who does not agree with me is a traitor.'

King George IV

b. 12 August 1762, d. 26 June 1830

Reigned 1820–30

GEORGE, the first monarch to inherit the new title King of the United Kingdom of Great Britain and Ireland, had been regent since 1811 due to his father George III's mental illness.

In 1785 George had secretly married a Catholic widow, but then in 1795 he also married Princess Caroline of Brunswick. A keen patron of the arts, George's reputation was undermined by his treatment of the popular Caroline. In 1820, George's divorce proceedings against his wife for adultery failed and caused a public outcry: in view of his infidelities, Caroline was seen as an unjustly persecuted woman. Her death the following year, combined with economic recovery, alleviated his reputation to some extent.

George IV's era saw the further gradual erosion in royal power. His ministers compelled him, for example, to repeal religious discrimination: the Catholic Relief Act was passed in 1829, permitting Catholics to become Members of Parliament.

George died in 1830 at Windsor Castle aged 67 without any surviving children, his daughter having died in 1817.

During George IV's reign, the National Gallery in London was established in 1824 and the Metropolitan Police Force set up by Robert Peel in 1829.

'If he ever had a friend – a devoted friend in any rank of life – we protest that the name of him or her never reached us.'

Times obituary

King William IV

b. 21 August 1765, d. 20 June 1837

Reigned 1830–37

WILLIAM, the third son of George III, succeeded his brother George IV aged 64. Despite his long affair with an actress, Mrs Jordan (with whom he had ten children), the early death of his brother's daughter and heir in 1817 led William to marry a Bavarian princess in 1818 to secure the succession.

Coming to the throne during a transfer of power from Tory to Whigs, and during the tense reform crisis, William helped facilitate the passage of the First Reform Act in 1832 which extended the vote. In 1835, the Municipal Reform Act required town councillors to be elected by ratepayers.

In his youth, William served in the Royal Navy in New York during the American War of Independence and hence was later known as the 'Sailor King'. George Washington allegedly agreed to a plot to have him kidnapped in 1782, although the plan was never enacted.

William died at Windsor Castle in 1837 without any surviving legitimate children.

During William's reign, slavery was abolished through-out the British Empire from 1833, a Factory Act in the same year prohibited young children working in factories, and a year later the Poor Law Act created workhouses for the poor.

'I have my view of things, and I tell them to my ministers. If they do not adopt it, I cannot help it. I have done my duty.'

Queen Victoria

b. 24 May 1819, d. 22 January 1901

Reigned 1837–1901

VICTORIA succeeded her uncle William IV in 1837 aged 18. She was the only child of Edward, Duke of Kent (fourth son of George III, r. 1760–1820). Edward's three elder brothers had all died, leaving no other surviving legitimate children. After Edward's death in 1820, Victoria was raised by her mother, Princess Victoria of Saxe-Coburg-Saalfeld, who supervised her strict upbringing very closely.

In 1840 Victoria married her first cousin Prince Albert of Saxe-Coburg-Gotha, who was to exert a tremendous influence over the Queen and her work. Left devastated after Albert's death in 1861, Victoria lived mostly in bereaved retirement.

Victoria's long reign spanned many key political, social and cultural changes in Britain, while the British Empire was further extended. Politically, her reign saw out numerous prime ministers, her relationship with them ranging from affectionate (Melbourne and Disraeli) to more stormy (Peel, Palmerstone and Gladstone). The Industrial Revolution transformed life, the 1884 Third Reform Act gave all adult males the vote and free schooling was introduced in 1891.

Her golden and diamond jubilees (1887 and 1897) helped counter some republican sentiment of the time.

Victoria died in 1901 aged 81 at her Isle of Wight home and was buried beside her beloved Albert in the Frogmore Mausoleum, Windsor.

'I am very young and … inexperienced, but I am sure that very few have more real good will and more real desire to do what is fit and right than I have.'

Extract from the Queen's Journal, 20 June 1837

HOUSE OF WINDSOR

1917–present

Following the House of Saxe-Coburg-Gotha (1901–17)

Windsor has been the official name of the royal family since 1917, when it was adopted in place of Saxe-Coburg-Gotha.

The German surname Saxe-Coburg-Gotha belonged to Queen Victoria's German-born husband, Prince Albert. Their descendants (Edward VII and George V) were therefore members of the House of Saxe-Coburg-Gotha, while Victoria was the final monarch of the House of Hanover.

However, when the First World War broke out in 1914, the German origins of the royal family became a source of embarrassment. So in July 1917, George V declared that all German titles would be renounced by the British royal family and the surname Windsor adopted. This proved popular despite the King's cousin, the German Kaiser, quipping about looking forward to 'The Merry Wives of Saxe-Coburg-Gotha'.

While Queen Elizabeth II's children might normally have taken their father's surname, Mountbatten, a royal proclamation in 1952 declared that her descendants would continue to bear the name Windsor. Since 1960, descendants of Queen Elizabeth II not entitled to be His/ Her Royal Highness (HRH) have borne the surname Mountbatten-Windsor.

The five monarchs of the House of Saxe-Coburg-Gotha which became the House of Windsor in 1917:

Edward VII (1901–10)

George V (1910–36)

Edward VIII (1936)

George VI (1936–52)

Elizabeth II (1952–present)

King Edward VII

Born into the House of Saxe-Coburg-Gotha;
changed to the House of Windsor in 1917 by George V
b. 9 November 1841, d. 6 May 1910

Reigned 1901–10

EDWARD (birth name Albert) was the eldest son of Queen Victoria and Prince Albert. Edward was a prominent socialite, whose skills as a future sovereign his parents doubted with some foreboding.

As Prince of Wales, Edward had many sporting interests, loved gambling and had numerous liaisons – the best known being Lillie Langtry, the 'Jersey Lily' – and was once even cited in a divorce case. In 1863 he married the graceful Princess Alexandra of Denmark, a steadying foil to his flamboyance and with whom he had six children. Edward toured India in 1875–76 while his mother, Empress of India, had never visited.

Ending a period of relative unpopularity abroad for Britain, especially during the Boer War of 1899–1902, Edward (together with Prime Minister Balfour) contributed to the Entente Cordial in 1904 with France and the Anglo-Russian agreement of 1907.

Edward died of pneumonia at Buckingham Palace in 1910, when it is said that his wife brought his current mistress, Mrs. Keppel, to his bedside to say her farewells.

During Edward's reign, the women's suffrage movement was founded, the fourth Olympic games were held in London in 1908 and the first cross-Channel flight from Calais to Dover took place in 1909.

'No, I shall not give in; I shall go on;
I shall work to the end.'

ON HIS LAST DAY, AFTER SEVERAL HEART ATTACKS

King George V

b. 3 June 1865, d. 20 January 1936

Reigned 1910–36

GEORGE, the second son, became heir following the death of his elder brother in 1892 and succeeded his father Edward VII. The following year, George married his deceased brother's formidable fiancée, Mary of Teck (later Queen Mary).

George was immediately plunged into handling a series of constitutional and political crises, which led to the 1911 Parliament Act curtailing the powers of the Lords to veto legislation.

His reign also covered foreign crises: the First World War (1914-18), which saw George make several visits to the frontline, and troubles in Ireland, which led to the creation of the Irish Free State and the province of Northern Ireland. His rule of almost 26 years spanned five prime ministers: Asquith, Lloyd George, Bonar Law, Baldwin and, in 1924, Ramsay MacDonald, the first Labour prime minister.

In 1917, George abandoned all German royal titles: the name of the royal house was changed from Saxe-Coburg-Gotha to Windsor.

George V died at Sandringham House in 1936. In an early display of media manipulation, Lord Dawson (the royal physician), is said to have given the ailing king a lethal dose of painkillers on his deathbed, so that the death would make the morning headlines rather than the 'less appropriate' evening ones.

'... the Old Country must wake up if she intends to maintain her old position of pre-eminence in her Colonial trade against foreign competitors.'

SPEECH AT GUILDHALL, 5 DECEMBER 1901

King Edward VIII

b. 23 June 1894, d. 28 May 1972

Reigned 1936

EDWARD, the eldest son of George V, succeeded to the throne on 20 January 1936. Before succession he had achieved genuine popularity with the public, spending time with the troops, visiting depressed areas and undertaking successful foreign tours. Able to communicate with ordinary people, he appeared a refreshing antidote to his austere and prudish parents, albeit that he made some statements, about a miner's relief fund, which some thought overstepped the non-political boundaries of a royal.

However, his 326-day reign was dominated within ruling circles by 'the King's matter'. Edward's intention to marry Mrs Wallis Simpson caused a constitutional crisis, with the public only becoming aware of it in December 1936. As an American and a divorcee with two husbands still living, Wallis would be unacceptable to the royal family and the Church.

On 10 December, Edward signed the Instrument of Abdication renouncing the throne for himself and his descendants. The couple left for France, where they were married the next year. The new king, Edward's younger brother George, agreed to award Edward the title Duke of Windsor. Later appointed Governor of the Bahamas (1940–45), Edward died in 1972 with Wallis passing away in 1986.

'I have found it impossible to … discharge my duties as King as I would wish to do without the help and support of the woman I love.'

ABDICATION SPEECH, 11 DECEMBER 1936

King George VI

b. 14 December 1895, d. 6 February 1952

Reigned 1936–52

GEORGE acceded to the throne unexpectedly on the abdication of his brother, Edward VIII in December 1936. Born Prince Albert and known as 'Bertie' to family and close friends, he was overshadowed by his brother Edward and was intensely shy, later developing a stammer.

In 1923 Prince Albert married Lady Elizabeth Bowes-Lyon, who provided much support during his reluctant and sudden accession. They were devoted parents to their two daughters, Elizabeth, the future monarch (b. 1926) and Margaret (b. 1930). In 1926, the future king George VI competed in the men's doubles tournament at Wimbledon.

Having inherited the steady virtues of his father George V, George VI overcame his shyness and became very popular with the public at a time when royal prestige was low due to the abdication crisis. In 1939 George announced the outbreak of the Second World War from Buckingham Palace. The royal couple refused to leave London and the two princesses spent much of the war at Windsor Castle.

Although a traditionalist, the King was not averse to the post-war social reforms of Attlee's Labour government. Regretting the loss of India to its independence in 1947, he strove to maintain Commonwealth ties. Aged 56, George died in 1952 at Sandringham House.

*'The highest of distinctions
is service to others.'*

Queen Elizabeth II

b. 21 April 1926

Reigned 1952–present

ELIZABETH succeeded to the throne aged 25 following the death of her father, George VI. The royal coronation in 1953 was the first seen on television, watched in huge numbers in austere, post-war Britain. Elizabeth had married her third cousin Philip Mountbatten in 1947, who after a lifetimes service, passed away just prior to his 100th birthday in April 2021. The strong sense of royal duty of the Windsor family, especially during the Second World War, had endeared them to the public and continued with the birth of their four children: Charles, Anne, Andrew and Edward.

However, a series of royal divorces, public rifts and press intrusions reduced royal reverence and saw the Queen declare 1992 to be an 'annus horriblis', while Princess Diana's death in 1997 saw republican sentiments voiced. A royal wedding in 2011 and the 2012 Diamond Jubilee has since helped restore popularity.

On 9 September 2015, Elizabeth II became Britain's longest-ever reigning monarch, surpassing Queen Victoria's reign of 63 years, 7 months and 2 days. Her long reign spans immense social, cultural, political and technological changes, from the world's first jet airliner service in 1952 to the digital dominance of today. Elizabeth II's rule has extended over 14 British prime ministers, from Churchill, Wilson, Thatcher and Blair to the present Boris Johnson, when the UK was confronted with the Coronavirus pandemic.

'I declare before you all that my whole life... shall be devoted to your service and the service of our great imperial family.'

ON HER 21ST BIRTHDAY, 21 APRIL 1947

CHARLES, PRINCE OF WALES

First in line to the throne

b. 14 November 1948

***Prince Charles**, the eldest son of Queen Elizabeth II and the Duke of Edinburgh, is heir to the British throne. He has been Duke of Cornwall and Duke of Rothesay since 1952, and was created Prince of Wales in 1958 (the longest-serving to hold that title).*

Charles became heir apparent aged 3, when his mother succeeded to the throne in 1952 aged 25. His education included Gordonstoun and Trinity College, Cambridge, earning a degree in history, before serving in the Royal Air Force and Royal Navy from 1971 to 1976. Contrary to modern royal convention, Charles has often voiced his opinions on social and environmental matters.

The first royal heir since 1660 to have an English wife, he married Lady Diana Spencer in 1981 and they had two sons: Prince William (b. 1982) and Prince Harry (b. 1984). Amidst much publicity around extramarital affairs, they separated in 1992 and divorced in 1996. His ex-wife Princess Diana died in a car crash in Paris in 1997 and Charles married his former girlfriend, Camilla Parker Bowles in 2005.

The Prince used his Navy severance pay – £7,400 – to fund a number of community initiatives, which became the founding projects of The Prince's Trust.

Prince Charles is the oldest and longest-serving heir apparent in British history.

'... a monstrous carbuncle on the face of a much-loved and elegant friend.'

On the proposed extension to the National Gallery, at the 150th anniversary of the Royal Institute of British Architects (RIBA), on 30th May 1984.

PRINCE WILLIAM, DUKE OF CAMBRIDGE

Second in line to the throne

b. 21 June 1982

***Prince William**, the eldest son of Prince Charles and the late Princess Diana, is second in line to the British throne after his father. Together with his younger brother Harry, William faced intense scrutiny from an early age following his parents' divorce in 1996 and then the death of his mother in 1997.*

William was educated at Eton College and the University of St. Andrews, graduating in 2005 with a geography degree. In 2006 he was commissioned in the Blues and Royals regiment, his service with the British forces ending in 2013. Since 2017, he has undertaken royal and charitable duties.

At university William met Catherine (Kate) Middleton, a 'commoner' with no royal lineage. William and Catherine were married on 29 April 2011 in Westminster Abbey and made Duke and Duchess of Cambridge. They are credited with helping to revive affection for the royal family. The Succession to the Crown Act was passed in 2013, taking away male bias in succession rules.

Prince George was born on 22 July 2013, becoming third in line to the throne, and was joined by Princess Charlotte on 2 May 2015 and Prince Louis on 23 April 2018.

'We had been talking about marriage for a while so it wasn't a massively big surprise. I took her up somewhere nice in Kenya and I proposed.'

INTERVIEW WITH WILLIAM AND KATE, 16 NOVEMBER 2010

PRINCE GEORGE OF CAMBRIDGE

Third in line to the throne

b. 22 July 2013

***Prince George** is the eldest son of Prince William and Catherine, Duchess of Cambridge. He is also the first great-grandson and third great-grandchild of the reigning monarch, Queen Elizabeth II. When George was born, he jumped the succession line ahead of his uncle Prince Harry.*

Just before George's birth, new rules on royal succession had been rushed through Parliament to remove male bias in succession rules. The Succession to the Crown Act 2013 ensured that if the Duke and Duchess had a baby girl, she would not be overtaken by any future younger brothers. George's arrival made him third in line to the throne even without the new legislation. George was later joined by siblings Charlotte (b. 2015) and Louis (b. 2018).

George was christened on 23 October 2013 by the Archbishop of Canterbury in St James's Palace, London. An historic photograph of the event included the current monarch Queen Elizabeth II with three future monarchs – her son Charles, grandson William, and great-grandson George– and echoed a similar image from Queen Victoria's reign capturing all the living heirs.

Having made his first foreign visit at eight months old, George started primary school in September 2017.

'George rules the roost and Charlotte isn't far behind.'

His father William, after George began full-time education

Although the author and publisher have made every effort to ensure that the information in this book was correct at time of printing, the author and publisher do not assume and hereby disclaim any liability to any party for any loss, damage, or disruption caused by errors or omissions, whether such errors or omissions result from negligence, accident, or any other cause.